Equivalence

SHIN YU PAI

EQUIVALENCE

for my APAWLI sister
Rosie,

with thanks for your
warmth & your teachings.
Shin Yu

La Alameda Press :: Albuquerque

Equivalence is the recipient of a
2003 grant from the Cambridge Arts Council
and the Massachusetts Cultural Council,
a state agency.

Cover painting:
Walker Buckner—*Landscape, New Zealand 11,*
2001, OIL ON WOOD
from the collection of John and Gail Harmon

Frontispiece:
Shin Yu Pai—*Chozubachi*
1999, SILVER GELATIN PRINT

ISBN: 1-888809-41-8

Library of Congress Cataloging-in-Publication Data

Pai, Shin Yu, 1975-
Equivalence / Shin Yu Pai.
p. cm.
ISBN 1-888809-41-8 (alk. paper)
I. Title.

PS3616.A3378E66 2003
811'.6--dc22

2003017298

La Alameda Press
9636 Guadalupe Trail NW
Albuquerque, NM 87114

For my parents
Tsu-Chiang and Noko Pai

Fall Aster with Firefly

A scroll passes hands in Chion-ji
street market, Kyoto
faded paper mounted over
homespun coarse dyed cotton
bands of brown and green
earth and moss,
a wet fox hair brush
dipped in ink and drawn
across paper one
hundred years ago
the image fanning outwards
a firefly at rest
pink aster blooms
swaying in wind
ichi go ichi e
one meeting one opportunity—
the months in which they courted
a season of fireflies
winged, nocturnal beetles
emitting a soft, bright light
brought home to hang
where incense burns
shake out the incense stick
this home lit by the heat
of fireflies

The Gathering at the Orchid Pavilion

Entering a darkened room
to pass between sixteen pillars
of equal height and depth,
ten feet high and one foot square,

I place my hand against the grain
hold my ear to a pillar
listening for something
like the sound of trees.

Across the room
six folded screens
colored ink and gold on silk

the specks of turquoise in those mountains
glimmering points of light
from a distance
the shine of moss

in memory like the lights
of houses in the hillsides
lanterns in the sea
of winter nights.

Mist erases crags and peaks.

Bearded scholars on blankets
read to one another
calligraphing poems
under shade of bamboo and plum

as servants fill cups
with rice wine
floated downstream
on lotus pads.

My breath clouds the casing
as I think of humidity
and the desire to touch things.

The door of the gallery opens.
A father and his daughter

I think we've seen this one before, the girl says.
They look for the place where the story begins.
The girl kisses the glass.

Where does the story begin?
Father insists gently.

In the mountains, the girl cries.

Traces of handprints left on the glass.

It starts here, she says
Here.

An Abbreviated History on the Way of Tea

The history of tea
nothing more than
a study of relations
between host and guest:

Sen-no-Rikyu expected a visit
from Daimyo Hideyoshi.
The evening preceding his arrival
a light snow fall.
The master lay cushions
on each stepping stone,
and upon the taiko's arrival
the garden covered
in a mantle of snow,
a path of stones standing out
to welcome him.

Frost on branches,
your arrival
in the garden.

Tracking the movement of seasons—
the placement of the hearth in winter
to offer you consolation from the cold.

Arranged in an earthen vase:
A branch of yellowed leaves,
a foxtail.

Water boiling
murmur of wind
through pine trees.

The knot on the wisk
pointing upwards.
A deviation from ceremony
a suggestion of desire
I could not articulate.

A scrap of paper
streaked with green
hidden in a sleeve
found hours after meeting.

Words fall from an envelope.

Melted wax
coats the interior
of a stone lantern.

Folding into an
overnight bloom,
the lovers.

Stars

(TANABATA POEM)

A strip of paper

knots and folds into a pentagon

collapsed body luminous pulp

u   n   r   a   v   e   l   s

a galaxy

between

Altair

and

Vega

Cormorant Fishing

Summer signified for 1,300 years
with the appearance of long boats
adrift along the Nagara River

paper lanterns illuminate the night
hand crafted from the interior bark
of mulberry trees, mino gami

stretched and fitted over bamboo frames—
the sculptor Isamu Noguchi called them
akari: weightless, light.

Night fishing for trout and ayu, the usho
stamps his feet on deck, his straw skirt stirs
a crew of cormorants

trained to dive on command
ten birds perched upon the helm
unleashed beneath the Ayu-no-se Bridge

entwined to their master by woven strands
of cypress encircling each bird's neck.
Reeled back on board

six fish pulled from one bird's throat
ten from another; the evening catch yields
forty pounds of iridescent fish

scales, silver glow on board the boat deck
refracting light transmitted through paper
lanterns illuminating an inner world.

The Pilot

you move through space
       in three dimensions
only in flight
       young,
a fascination starts
       with the push off
the third story of a neighbor's roof
       and the desire to explore
what tooth and hip remember
       more clearly than a father tells it
       falling
       crack of bone
disruptions to water
in   inner
       the   ear
how the body compensates
       for fractures
by honing
       situational awareness
based on
       career vocation
you have perfect eyesight
       at night
low level cargo flights
       over the Persian sea
the belt of Orion
       in the Northern hemisphere
or
       a belt of military ships
orthogonal lines recede into a space
       where boats to you are as stars

It Was a Clear Moonlit Night
(or How the Moon Got Its Rhythm)

Knocked from sky
            a full and laughing moon
sole witness to a dumpling theft
            by greedy god
Ganesh
            earth and umbra
the fragmentation of
            lunation
reinvocation of light
            and the restoration of
the lunar cycle:
            twenty nine days, twelve hours
forty four minutes
            and 2 .8 seconds
between successive moons
            puncture wound
maculations, bowl-shaped
            depressions of craters
crescent shaped
            elephant tusk
new moon,
            echo
of old laughter

True or False

water on the eye's surface freezes at ten below zero

wild green Argentine parrots nest in the sumac trees of
                                        Hyde Park

the Milky Way galaxy is a gathering of magpies

summer nights lightning bugs hover over blue stem

a medicinal brew of bees in wine eases ailments of the liver

cabbage extract in red grapefruit juice causes depression
                                        in O-positive carriers

potatoes, corn, and yellow bell peppers are genetically
                                        engineered hybrids

scratches around the keyhole of a painted door record the
                                        passage of time

the common dictionary, a tool of divination

rock candy arrived in Japanese teahouses via Portugal

black tea substitutes for chemical toner in photo-processing

the process of red blood cells combating white blood cells
                                        translates as health

toxins in his body slowly bleached his eyes from brown to blue

flat footed men avoid the draft, but suffer from lack of support

the rings inside a redwood point north

Things Which Give Pleasure

The fifty franc bill bearing the image of Le Petit Prince.

A handsome stranger gives up his seat for you on the metro.

Tapas, sushi, carrot cake.

Chanel No. 5.

Friday night date at the Metropolitan Museum of Art with one
you adore. Rodin sculptures: Cupid and Psyche, The Kiss.
Modigliani portraits, long heads and no eyeballs.

Pablo Neruda read aloud by a native Spanish speaker.

Eating violets hand-picked from the lawn by a friend,
remembering Easter cake garnished with purple blossoms.

The lunar new year, a new suit of clothes, and a haircut.

Spring day: licorice root tea shared with a curly-haired boy.
He brews it in a pot for you. Who cares if neither of you can
afford a kettle?

Open Me Carefully

kettle and cross-stitch,
the purposeful act of   .
making a precise thing,
measure, mark and score
each page, each distance
between words and
rhyme, bound, but unboxed
a thread connecting forms
still uncontained

hand bound booklets
side stabbed and sewn together
pages nested firmly into one
another, the way things fit,
death, desire and Sunday hymns,
painstakingly bound *fascicles*
stacked in a clothes drawer
discovered in your room—
a bundle of pine needles

cut the tie
and unknot the bow
to gather and fasten
together your own
signatures,

        your own,
        strange Emily

Recipe for Paper

FOR ANDREW SCHELLING

I.

Send legal briefs, failed attempts at love
letters and other confidential documents
through a shredder,

soak over night in a warm bath,

scoop handful of wet paper
into kitchen blender add
boiled daffodil stems,

mashed into a pulp, then blend
black tea leaves, garlic
or onion skin,

translucent stains
of color,

pulp until smooth as oatmeal
in a plastic tub combine
one part pulp to three parts water

II.

A closely guarded secret for centuries until the T'ang Dynasty,
when on the banks of the Tarus River, Islamic warriors overtook a
caravan traveling on the Silk Road, spiriting Chinese prisoners away
to Samarkand. Their lives spared in exchange for sharing their secret
with the Western world. Samarkand fast became a paper-making
capital and the practice of slaughtering three hundred sheep to make
a single sheet of parchment hide quickly became a thing of the past.

The addition of crushed spices creates a textured surface to the
paper, as do crumbled tea leaves, coffee grounds, and dried flowers.
When a freshly pulled sheet of paper is pressed beneath a warm
steam iron, the fragrance of these organic materials is slowly
released into the air.

Before the invention of paper the sutras were incised into cave walls,
verses from Lao Tzu's *Tao Te Ching* painted on silk. In ancient China,
Tsai L'un, Director of the Imperial Office of Instrument and
Weapons, won the favor of the emperor. By pounding the branches
of mulberry trees and husking bamboo with a wooden mallet,
Tsai L'un discovered the method of separating plant filaments into
individual fibers. Mixed with water and poured into a vat, a screen
of bamboo reeds was submerged into the suspension. The tangle
of pulp floating to the water's surface and trapped on top of the
mold resulted in a thin layer of interwoven fibers. Drained, pressed,
and hung to dry—the birth of "Tsai ko-shi."

The history of paper contained within a mulberry bark and seed,
the paper on which these words are printed.

The poet should consider this story with care throughout the years.

H

The source of the argument originated in a printshop with two working sets of typeface: Garamond and Palatino. One set lacked the consonant "H," the other lacked the letter "A." The type-setter, an admirer of Rimbaud, looked to the poet's work on vowels to determine which letter held more intrinsic value. Using Palatino to set the type, the typesetter avoided and edited out words from the text like phlebotomy and thanatos.

Later, a language theorist develops a hypothesis for why "H" should be removed from the twenty-six letters of the alphabet. A lack of auditory appeal—the push of sound straight from the throat. Useful for vocalists exercising the larynx and other organs of respiration. Still, even for a practicing singer, the consonant serves the vowel as a starting point to strike the bell upon breathing. The absence of the sacred, or holy. A lack of heart, and the elimination of ghazal causing a certain weltschmerz of idea in opposition to reality which can only be termed depression, though still the suggestion of "H," if not in breath, than in exhalation.

An Explanation of Magic

Who you envision coming into your life rarely resembles what
you imagine. The object of desire collects bugs, has a food allergy
to shellfish, maybe citrus fruit (but not cabbage), or has taken
vows of monasticism. So few ideals smell of lilac or are heralded
by flocks of yellow butterflies.

At the Why Not Café where they meet for dinner, he tells her,
"It's as simple as this glass of water." She chews on a grilled
cheese sandwich and watches hard. "I concentrate all my mental
energy on moving this glass from Point A to Point B." He
squeezes his eyes shut and wiggles his fingers, opens his eyes
and scrutinizes the table for changes. "It's neither the seen nor
the unseen, mathematical equations nor illusions." He removes
his spectacles and lights another cigarette. "Would you move
that glass for me?" She picks up the glass and moves it to the
edge of the table.

Kites

vibrate

and ring

across

the sky

set free,

dispel illness

poor luck

the battle

lost

or

signal

help

lazy

swimming

the

backstroke

strung

along

to fly

a kite

to hold

the wind

between

two hands

Blauer Himmer

Phillip's melancholy over returning to Berlin after living in Santa Barbara, stemmed from a lack of blue sky there. "Always grey like sidewalks," and yet, a place called home. Paul checks the weather reports in Berlin daily. He writes a postcard to Phillip in which he copies out

" blauer himmer blauer himmer blauer himmer
   blauer himmer blauer himmer blauer himmer
   blauer himmer"

The postcard's picture: blue and cumulus. Paul chants "blauer himmer" one hundred times while dancing beneath the sky. Phillip writes to Paul a month later, "Tuesday, last week all the people stopped and came out of their houses …"

Color Study

I.

A tube of Windsor's Yellow Ochre can not substitute for the density of pine or buttercup pollen, in the way that a plastic filter can not replicate the deepest hues of the sky. As a reminder to herself to always question her relationship to color, she kept a postcard of New Mexico on her desk. An old adobe church in Chimayo silhouetted against the sky, clouds rolling overhead. Her experiences of landscape as a traveler had been of clay and dust, the color red and on occasion yellow.

II.

When she was young, she played a game called Memory with her brother, in which they flipped over cardboard squares laid out in a grid. They matched images of birds and automobiles, telephones and umbrellas. Her brother, the strategist, devised his own associations, assigning numbers to each revealed image to make calculated choices. She would look for the sound of a rotary phone and wonder why tomatoes corresponded to red when red had more in common with umbrellas.

III.

Slowly, blue edged out the yellow in her photographs, as she tried
to replicate the color scale of the sky over the Southwest. She
found the solution to manipulating the surfaces by pushing one
color to take over another. All the pictures before had been of
yellow: goldfish, bell peppers, and wheat fields. Still she could
never photograph yellow without thinking of small children or
the rain. Now the photographs were of peacock and delphinium.
She wanted more naturally occurring blue objects. She needed
more imagination. She could name more than three if she counted
eggplant and hypothermia.

Freehand

The master draftsman ordained
a method of seeing plums
visualize Handel's fugues
moving in step
patterns across a page
black dots ascending
and descending
in minute intervals

breathe,
        animate,
light
        and eye
                falling
                    across an object
pay most mind to line
drawn with short strokes;
train accuracy,
repeating this simple pattern—
flushed red plum
on newsprint
swells into shadow
forgives your imitation,
lumpy tuber contours,
lacking value,
pretend a different plum
would be easier to draw
Why draw plums at all,
how about bananas?

Feedback
AFTER JOHN POMARA

the   push   and   p   u   l   l
          of paint   sliding across a surface
 rolling tremolo machine
paint flows off
the hard edge of aluminum
          Rohrschach drips
read on the horizontal:

a   graph   body's
                         of the   progress
stut-ter-ing
on the vertical—
a
screen-
play
glitches
on
8 mm
race
across
a
film
strip
shifting
             cut up
                              xerox
magnified
             blow up

d r a g g e d across an electric eye
emanations of light from behind the screen
                    the absence of painter
                                        presence of machine
the television a template
                    for a sketch enacted
in childhood
                    boxes full of light
reaching through the screen
                    the human hand
                                        leaves its traces

A Conversation between Huidobro and Braque

Is a poem a poem?
And isn't an orange just an orange,
and not an apple?

Yet next to each other, the orange
ceases to be orange
the apple ceases to be apple,
and together the two
become fruit.

Milkstone

the splash and spread
        of milk poured over stone
                like paint applied to wet
watercolor paper
        the slow bleed to edge
                milk on Macedonian marble
tension of liquid on solid
        surface
                purer than pigment
laid over unprimed
        canvas by Robert Ryman
                caked with paint,
white on white,
        a circle of milk poured
                and pulled into a square
finger drawn milk
        mandala
                to flood the gates
turn a finger inwards
        throwing a glance
                the Buddha lifted a finger
in a crowd of thousands
        gesture overflowing
                fullness
liquid trails gliding
        into seamless, trembling
                being

Number 14

interlaced lines of
black, silver, and white

moonlight woven
dense as tree branches

the primordial visual
field on Long Island

Sound, seashells washed
up on the seashore,

reordered by tides
no man before

Pollock to turn
a gaze downwards,

gardening pictures,
rooting contact,

glimpses of white
show through canvas,

light falling through
slats in a barn roof,

patterns tesselate,
reiterate and repeat

a fractal dimension
hurled dripped flung

and come full circle to
galaxy and coastline,

you designed no
beginning, middle,

end, when
you said

I am *nature.*

Poem

FOR WOLFGANG LAIB

a life
of collecting pollen
from hazelnut bushes
a life of gathering word-grains
to find all you have wanted
all you have waited to say

five
mountains
we cannot climb
hills we cannot touch
perhaps we are only here
to say house, bridge, or gate

a passage
to somewhere else
yellow molecules
spooned and sifted
from a jar filled with

sunlight
          pouring
milk
          over
                    stone
you are the energy
that breaks form
building wax houses
pressed from combs

a wax room
set upon a mountain
an offering of rice
nowhere everywhere
the songs of Shams

                    m

          u
                         p
J

The true self revealed
          while the mind meditates
upon the act of jumping
          forgets the shutter release
the photographer beneath the
          black cloth
a theory of jumpology
endorsed by famed celebrities
          Tallchief
          Monroe
          Astor
          and
          Ford
the subject focuses upon two factors:
height and
          landing
caught
          mid-air
Halsman's most famous shot
          a print
after twenty-
                    three
choreographed takes

      painter Salvador Dalí
equipped with brush and canvas
         buckets of water stream across   the frame
as black cats fly   across
            a white backdrop
      thrown from the margins
feline, aqueous, ephemeral
      the primal, elemental, and human
aspects of a face you wore
      before you were born
      leaping
      into void   (READER JUMPS FROM CHAIR WHILE READING LAST LINE)

Reel

spin and tilt
        your rib cage
of vaulted bone
        shadow arcs
tunnel shaft
        vertebral
    discs
arcing near
        enough to touch
another galaxy

the earth tilts
        its axis
with greater speed
        than the click of a camera lens
a shutter closing
        the human eye
                blinks
missing
        light years elapsed
through the exposure of film
        the photograph
a document of the time
        it took to push
youth through adolescence
        forcing amaryllis bulbs
in the garden
        an explosion of
light rays
across your body

freckle patch
      star cluster
blur
 of sunburnt
childhood
neither pain
 nor quiet pleasure
 in the shedding of membrane
but tenderness for each

De Stijl

blocks of color
move across canvas
syncopated
      revisionist
divisionism—
a method of placing blue
   alongside yellow
to signify green
Seurat's influence
in Mondrian's early work:
the windmill at Blaricum
Dutch landscape painting
and years spent rendering chrysanthemums
collecting
images from nature
a subsequent progression
from reality to abstraction
rectangular planes
and the repetition of elements
red
blue
white
yellow
black
~~lines drawn, crossed out,~~
~~and drawn again~~
lines drawn, crossed out,
and drawn again

        to add more
boogie
woogie
dissonant
            harmony
measures of blue
            on the downbeat

Heart-Shaped Box

of dream-
(e)scapes, desire
hinged, your heart
opens and closes
a romantic ballet or play
the stage set:
a backdrop of night—
cut and paste down
the constellations,
navigational tools for
men lost at sea,
handmade valentines
for starlets and girls
never kissed but still
dreamed of
marked return to sender,
Utopia Parkway,
to give one's self
over to desire,
a gamble like
shooting marbles
or slot machines
registering
girl
cherry
bell
Easter eggs come
rolling out of France
when you ring me,
candy-hearted, chalklike

crumble and breakup
on re-entry
I dream you in another orbit
in museums where each
emptiness, every cavity
filled by cherry soda
and chocolate cake,
birds nesting in abandoned
dovecotes

Groundwind

basalt: hard, igneous
rock hurled
from volcanos

formed from feldspar,
augite, magnetite,
the unexpected gathering of

force, let
material give
birth to form

the sculptor pictures
the movements of tea,
the reversal of lightness

into substance, heavy
as a bamboo
scoop lifted

with the care of
a cast iron kettle handled
with perfect ease

current of air, zero
of potential, wind made
solid as stone

Equivalent

At an exhibition of Felix Gonzales-Torres
black and white
        clouds on paper
                bleed to edge
the slow drift and pull
        of clouds soaring across the horizon
                weather forecast
over Stieglitz's Lake George
        overcast with breaking
                thundershowers
poster sheets
        stacked half a foot high
                the removal of cloud layers
from cube
        reshaping
                the whole—
What you touch,
        take
                with you
a piece of hard green candy
        pulled from a spill
                on the gallery floor,
portrait of a friend
        the qualities he gave those
                he loved
transposed into sweet pile,
        please keep
                with you
this sweetness,
        passing

Poem for Art Handlers

Start from square one:
21 isometric cubes of varying sizes
with color ink washes superimposed
guidelines for a wall drawing,
a written instruction, intangible
scribbled notes and diagrams

find creative storage solutions—
three thousand pounds of Belgian
candies imported for a Gonzales-Torres
exhibition to be stored on the delivery
dock or held in low humidity
alongside Cannaletto?

if only we hadn't sprayed the crickets
raining from the ceilings, clogging
the elevator shafts, one step up
on the evolutionary food chain above
wingless insects feeding on the pollen
fields, engorged bugs leaving their tracks

wire a phone jack in the east gallery
and wait for Yoko to call
she will telephone and tell you
to imagine a happening where
you clock out early after
letting loose at closing

a herd of starving cats
converging to lap up milk
pooling on a marble stone

Yes Yoko Ono

—

STONES

Remove a stone from an unmarked pile.
Choose one pile to add it to—
a mound of joy
or a mound of sorrow.
Or take a stone from a mound of sorrow
and move it to a mound of joy.

二

PAINTING TO LET THE EVENING LIGHT COME THROUGH

Lift the blind of the bedroom window.
Place a clear glass bottle
on the window sill.
The painting exists when
the stars have risen.

三

PAINTING FOR THE WIND

Write down your favorite words
on separate scraps of paper.
Leave the paper where there is wind.
The scraps of paper can be lottery receipts,
business cards, or paper napkins.

四

PAINTING TO HAMMER A NAIL

Hammer a nail into a mirror.
Place the pieces
in an abandoned lot
with an unobstructed view of
the sky.

五

PAINTING TO BE CONSTRUCTED IN YOUR HEAD

Imagine a painting.
Cut out colors, shapes, and things you like.
Paste them on a blank background.
Cover the whole thing in a wash of white,
or whatever is your favorite color.

Sheep piece

Borrow a herd of sheep,
one hundred in number or more
spray paint their fleece
with your favorite words.
Watch from a distance as the sheep
arrange themselves into poems.

七

HOUSECLEANING PIECE

Remove all the light
bulbs from the fixtures.
When night has fallen
organize your things
into boxes.

Circle, Triangle, Square

when Sengai put brush to paper
he drew three forms, overlapping
square, triangle, circle

a koan for disciples
for scholars to argue and
decipher throughout the ages

the temple walls are four-
sided within them sit
and practice

upon achieving a mind
of enlightenment, see
the circle, an empty teaching

the trinity,
and the confines of
earth-bound existence, *or*

circle
triangle
square

a lesson
in geometry
intended for children

A Fly Lands on the Great Eastern Sun

After what feels as if
surely lifetimes of sitting—
(*poor* meditator of five years)
I raise my gaze
and glimpse a fly landed
on the Great Eastern Sun,
what had been only
a golden circle of silk
wrinkled, rippling edges
like heat wave,
sun burning on the horizon
optical illusion
sewn on to a field of white.
In the meditation hall
a banner hung high
upon the wall
becoming
oranges heaped
upon the shrine
musca domestica
enshrined in a bar
of amber
six insect legs
buzz
          blaze
across
          surface of sun

Meditation on Frank O'Hara

It's March 16, 1999
and I'm walking down Washington
and the clock on the Leumi Bank
tells me it's 10:25 in Hebrew
whereas time has stopped altogether
in Mayor Ogden Plaza,
the arms of the motorized Vito Acconci
tied at twelve
granite numbers relegated
to pedestrian benches
and I'm passing through Daley Plaza
noticing for the first time the Joan Miró
across from the Picasso
the scale of a hunched over elderly woman
resting at the sculpture's stone base
and I see Icarus, not on the Rue Montparnasse
as in Jack Greene's poem
a feather on the grate
but at the entrance of La Salle bank
across from which city hall celebrates the holiday
by spraying water the color of artificial shamrocks
from the plaza fountain,
St. Patrick's Day years ago
when I was sullen and anemic
a girl in public school
too stubborn to wear green
the option of getting punched or kissed
still one and the same
and I walk to the Cultural Center
where a woman asks to see my ID when I apply for a job

and I haven't yet committed to living in Chicago
as my driver's license reflects,
grown accustomed to a city
where big shoulders refers to meat packers
instead of shoulder pads or beautiful men
and outside in the plaza
children slide down the face of the Picasso

Sainte Terrer

The pale head of a freshly shaved monk
equipped with sunblock
extra shoelaces and begging bowl
thankful for all offered
tablescraps, carrottops
and the occasional dismembered finger
learning unattachment from a strict vegan diet.

On your left wrist a wooden mala
eighteen beads of sanded cedar on elastic cord
one hundred and eight incantations
of *om mani padma hum*
each bead a benefactor
who has sponsored a leg of the journey
from Boulder to Tassajara.

Roving about the countryside
as in the Middle Ages
on the pretense of traveling
a la Sainte Terre
the Holy Land.
Children called you "Sainte Terrer,"
Saunterer, or Holy-Lander
erasing your tracks in dust.

Peregrination
the migratory urge to be as birds
a practice centuries old
handed down from master to disciple
a genetic trace this compulsion
for flight.

An inability to remain quietly in a room
why you are compelled in movement
the continuum of ancestors and totems
the walking details of earth—
If you don't like to step on thorns and rocks
as you walk around the planet
you can pave the entire earth with shoe leather
or you can make a pair of sandals.

Wash, Cut and Dry

Christina and Alec had a ritual of going to the barbershop together. In part, this was for Alec's vanity that his lover should ever cut her long, flowing hair more than a requisite few inches to remove the dead ends. On the day in which she'd made the appointment, the network crashed at his office, and Alec worked late into the night to repair the system. Christina went alone to see Mario in his shop—the old man, with brown eyes and liverspotted hands, massaged her scalp with lemon-scented soap. She rested in his chair thinking if he asked her if she wanted to try something new, she would answer, "yes."

The Baptism

His parents planned the event for the Saturday afternoon preceding Easter. Relatives and friends gathered to attend the ceremony, which was to be held outdoors, at the Grand Forks River. Wren went underwater and came up, only to find that the minister had disappeared. The sun was bright, the guests were laughing, and his parents shook their heads, asking, "Does it count?" While submerging Wren, the minister had apparently slipped on a rock and gone under. Years later, his parents were not surprised to hear he had become a Buddhist.

Monasticism

Aside from their contribution to population control, her under-
standing of monks was constantly shifting. She met him outside
the Methodist chapel giving away copies of *The Bhagavad Gita*. He
had just moved to the city and was boarding at the ISKCON
temple where he worked as a kitchen aide, which meant rising
earlier than four a.m. chants to "Hare Krishna". Intrigued by his
lifestyle, she visited the temple to hear a lecture on the *Gita*. It was
snowing on her path to the brownstone, where she hung her coat
and removed her boots, placing them alongside dozens of shoes.
Across the room, against the wall a bronze statue of Swami
Prabhuphada, founder of ISKCON. The myth surrounding
Prabhuphada tells of his arrival to the United States on a steamer
boat with a tin of betel nut and a tubercular condition. The
lecture on the *Gita* concluded, and several peach and grey robed
monks cleared a space on the hardwood floor, pulling lay people
and children into their circle to join in dancing. She found herself
looking around the room at images of blue Krishnas to find that
the statue of Prabhupada near the entry had been swaddled in
blankets, with an electric space heater placed at its feet. Later, she
had opportunity to approach an apprentice monk in grey and ask
why men and women did not dance together during the ritual
ceremony. Sweating and animated from dancing, the young novice
replied, "We are monks. We get excited when we dance with
girls."

Tea with Omar

Ten minutes of zazen is followed by tea service, in the shrine room of the Karma Dzong. The tea, boiling hot, does not affect any of the meditators. The practitioners gulp it down and dry their cups, returning to sitting posture. I whisper to my friend Omar, "I'm not done yet." Eyeing the four sips of tea that remain in the bottom of my cup, I realize there is little possibility that the tiny cloth square used to dry the ceramic will absorb the remaining liquid. Omar calmly, "Drink it." The umdze scowls and I finish, not tasting a drop, as I envision getting whacked with a stick by T'ang Master Ma-tsu.

The ceremony comes to an end and the leader of the Rinzai group offers his private instruction. He says the sound of Omar's breathing is too labored, which amuses me, as I had failed to notice anything except for the growling of a stomach to my left. At sunrise that morning, I'm busy tracking the reflection of the orange blinds in the lacquered floor. Some blue zafu cushions are extremely flat while others appear plump and unused. I envision heavy and thin practitioners meditating in all postures. During the walking portion of the morning practice, the texture of Omar's corduroy pants are endearing. Later, we realize we forgot to turn our teacups upside down.

Instant Karma

Some friends and I work a dinner for a touring Rinpoche at a private residence in the mountains. While searching for a place to store our coats, I open the door to the meditation room, a converted walk-in closet. The hostess sits before a thangka of the Buddha, cross-legged in meditation. The smell of sandalwood and sagebrush permeates the room. *Jesus!* she exclaims.

Emerging from the closet twenty minutes later, she warns us to be careful when handling the dishware, as at their last party, a long-stemmed glass tipped with gold was damaged by the "help." The three-course meal is to be served on china plates hand-painted with a rustic New England log cabin scene. The chef prepares pot roast, green beans, and herbed potatoes for the evening's repast. *Not all Buddhists, (Tibetans in particular), are vegetarian, because it is difficult to grow anything in Tibet,* he explains.

This Rinpoche also takes a liking to Steven Segal movies. The host of the party has procured copies of *Hard to Kill* and *Marked for Death* as a gift for the teacher. Segal has been recently named the reincarnation of Kyung-drak Dorje, meaning that he can no longer appear in movies committing acts of violence. The Rinpoche arrives forty-five minutes late in a tight fitting suit, flanked by two young, blond female attendants.

They scarcely taste their food and the leftovers of the guru are saved to be offered to the dead at the family shrine in the woods. Before the leftovers leave the table, each of the guests is permitted a drink from the Rinpoche's glass insuring the improvement of personal karma and good health. As I wash dishes at the sink, Camilla slips back into the kitchen with a piece of biscuit the

Rinpoche hid in his napkin. I steal a bite when no one is looking. Later, I feel extremely ill. Towards the end of Rinpoche's visit, the host brings us out of the kitchen to introduce us to Rinpoche. That is, he presents Rinpoche and forgets our names. Rinpoche shakes our hands and bows graciously.

A week later, I dream of Chogyam Trungpa Rinpoche, founder of the Buddhist college. He is stern with me wagging his finger and shaking his head, warning, *Do not speak poorly of your teachers.*

Office Feng Shui

A specialist is brought in to the Buddhist college to redirect the
negative energy flowing from the tail of the dragon through
Arapahoe Avenue, and into the corner suite of the main office.
He rearranges the furniture, and everything red is removed. Red,
the color of padma, manifests as passion in its neurotic state and
draws out the existing energy in a field. The staff member in the
room closest to the street is removed from her office, which has
been marked with two 2's, the number of disease. ($2 + 2 = 4$, the
Chinese number of death. But not quite that serious, according to
the specialist.) He prescribes fish. Fish, the symbol for prosperity
and good luck, will absorb the negativity. Since real fish would die
in the windowsill, the specialist brings in a miniature tank of
hand-painted magnetic fish. The bands of orange and red on the
fish have been carefully concealed with blue and yellow acrylic
paint. To maintain fake fish: Reach a hand into the aquarium
when the fish stop swimming clump and together, grab the fish by
their tails, and shake the bubbles from their bodies.

Mosaic

The fiancé with the exotic dishware fetish broke their engagement to go on tour with experimental noise band Gova Gojiva. Lee played some guitar, but his main instrument was dishes— spinning them in air and breaking pottery. On her days off from the restaurant she found herself wandering the housewares department of the Marshall Field's where they had registered. She roamed the aisles between Mikasa and Lladro, running her fingertips along the imported ceramic. She decided it was time for a vacation. Looking through color brochures of Barcelona, she comes across the architecture of Anton Gaudi, his Catedral de la Sagrada Familia, an one hundred year long project. She finds photographs of his park benches in the Parc Guell, miles of benches snaking around the perimeter of a public park, embedded with tile and glass. She imagines the hundreds of dishes she has carried over the years and pictures smashing each one to bits. She leaves waitressing to join the production line of a ceramics manufacturer where she grouts terracotta planters and birdbaths eight hours a day. Shortly thereafter, she makes her first sale at an uptown gallery—bits of her fiancé's favorite percussion instruments reassembled.

Fruit They Had in Common

He was convinced that you had to eat the entire thing in one sitting. A condition of childhood and a grandmother who served watermelon to the grandchildren entrusted to her care, as meal (breakfast, lunch, *and* dinner), in between her requests of stirred martinis and service in bed. He remembers reading a haiku by a Japanese poet in which a farmer invokes a spell upon his water-melon patch. When thieves approach at night to steal the fruit, the watermelons transform into frogs and escape. As a boy, he often wished that the watermelon on his plate would come alive and hop away.

She had her own memories of summer fruit—an ama who educated her in maintaining a balanced diet of hot and cool foods. During the hot season, Grandmother insisted she rub the white of the rind over her face until sticky and wet. She had a theory concerning cool foods and their absence in the diet of prominent government leaders—for instance, if the Chinese would only eat more carrots it would cool their ardor for con-quering foreign nations and erasing history.

A Type of Fish

Lost in translation, everything becomes a "type of fish." A young American visiting her father's family in Taiwan for the first time, eyes the main course suspecting mollusks, crustaceans, sea cucumbers, and any other underwater life fall under the category of "type of fish." The following day, her uncle takes her to Taichung harbor to walk through the largest fishmarket in the city. He points out the various incarnations of what she has consumed over the course of their last few days in Ching Shui. He stops to choose from piles of dried fish, tiny silver flakes with lidless black eyes. Her uncle converses with the boyish fishmonger who grabs sardines by the handful, scattering silver everywhere. He shoves them into a clear plastic bag and weighs them on the electronic scale, divulging with a conspiratorial smile that the fish were netted off the coast of Hong Kong. "Then they should be cheaper!" her uncle complains. In another part of the market, a merchant displays a chain of black-shelled crabs—the claws of each crab bound with red ribbon and laced to every other crab in the metallic container. As she bends to examine one of the small captives more closely, its eyeballs retract into its head and she is reminded of the turtle living in the porcelain sink of the downstair's bathroom in her uncle's house which she always hopes to catch off guard before it pulls its head back into its shell.

Transience

—

She writes to him while traveling the South East coast, en route to Taipei Railway Station—*Passengers on a train preoccupy themselves with sitting in seats facing the direction of travel.* There are individuals who complain of motion sickness, when unable to see ahead to a point of destination. Those unlucky enough to face backwards, sleep, creating diversion. Sunlight and betel nut trees float past the window. Fragments of dreams make their way across the countryside.

That night, a rock concert and the celebration of the new year in Chiang-kai Shek Memorial Plaza. Recollections of Morgan Neiman, a friend from foreign geographies, who described her life in Sevilla as being "outdoors a lot." She imagines boarding an airplane home, crossing time zones and meridians to see him again. In the morning, telecasts of celebrations in the States. Times Square, a falling ball of light. The tradition of kissing strangers.

二

One morning, she rides the El into the city. Business men crowd
the aisles with briefcases. Raincoats, umbrellas, sweat. She looks
up from his letter long enough to rest her eyes out the window. In
Kyoto, it is tomorrow. *Haru*, the commencement of a new season.
The train plunges beneath ground, a shift from light to dark—
the speed of a single film frame. White faces reflected in the
blackness of windows, expressions softened by steam. The hour
she wakes, the hour he sleeps. Life a dream, lasting until death,
where fears and regrets are as unreal as desire.

The Customer

Maybe he has waited tables too
       she imagines
              clearing away the dishes
noticing the generous tip
       long after he disappeared
              out the front door
in a windbreaker
       illsuited for New England Octobers.
The sidewalk cafes
       have begun an early retreat
              and it has been a hectic day
on the floor.
       He ordered chef's salad
              and she left him
with two translucent bottles
       of vinegar and oil
              only to discover later that
the oil which oozed
        from the bottle
             on to the half-eaten
bed of lettuce
       had been honey!
Earlier that morning
       a customer commented
              to her companion,
on the service:
       At the deli haus
              every day is training day.

Certain,
        she had kept *him*
                waiting
bringing the bill
        a quarter of an hour
                past finishing,
though he never mentioned her mistake
        left behind a drawing
                on a paper napkin
a playful sketch in pencil
        of a muted figure
                delivering plates
pouring coffee
        taking orders
                with caption
—*a busy day at the deli haus*

Feed

trapped between a rock
and a fat place, if I turn
down the other half of
that macaroon, you are
fool to believe it a rejection
any more serious than a
refusal of the statement

"I want to see you eat
that french fry," you said to
me, and what I wanted to say to
you: the body not the gift of
good genetics or random selection
but the product of a mind—
not the hamburger but a

relationship to addiction,
binge and purge, a ten mile
dash for every three pounds
gained, a case of the runs
in place, going nowhere
a Muybridge photo, study of
how the human body works

to make up for never-ending
fad diets—low carb, raw food,
protein, and ephedra, counting
points not calories, you eat
your maximum quota for a week

within an hour, comfort yourself
with crawling into bed where

you blackout dreaming,
of all the delicacies placed
before you that you will devour;
an "edible complex," like rats
eating their young, I wouldn't
put past you this biological
obsession with hunger

World vs. Bromberg

I read in the newspaper of
a dispute between neighbors:
Lynn and Richard Bromberg
are denied a permit to build
a new front door on their newly
purchased Brookline townhouse.

The Bromberg's neighbors, Che Jianme
and Yan Xiaowei, long-time residents
of the La Grange Street community claim
the new front door would face the
entrance of their own home, and
violate the principles of feng shui—

the philosophy of living *with*
versus *against* nature—
creating disharmony by sucking
any positive energy out of
the Che and Yan household
and into the Bromberg home.

Hoping for dialogue and peaceful
resolution between neighbors,
the city Board of Appeals
denies the building permit.

The injured party is quoted
as denouncing "those people's"

beliefs, as "voodoo" in a front
page story announcing multiple
lawsuits filed against both
city and neighbor.

Trappings

An old man
crossing the street
pushes two

shopping carts
brimming with things—
one cart lashed

behind the other
with a rope long
enough to hang

a man, unwashed
and graying, pushes
forward, as the other

sways behind
back and forth,
countering traffic

Trompe l'Oiel

cold
        snap—

the last
snow of

spring
outlines

the tops
of branches

against
dull skies,

draw
the eye

in
closer

even
the word

icicle

carries
its

connotations
of death

Angel from Mexicali

Teeth so white
he could eat lemons every day
never a thought wasted
on the brightness of his smile.

March

The composer
taped himself jogging
shoes slapping
concrete
in the Czech Republic
rhythm
for a new composition.

Dog Story

When grandfather
died, father's dog,

refused to eat
for eight days,

howling through eight
nights. Finally,

third uncle tied
a black ribbon

around the dog's leg,
identical to the arm-

bands each family
member wore.

How To Eat Sugarcane

You buy stalks
of roasted
sugarcane
in the night market
blackened over
charcoal
ends protruding past the grill.
A vendor chews betel nut;
red saliva stains
the pavement.
His rusted machete blade
pares back the hardened shell
to white pulp and flesh.
Guava and carambola—
fruit we share in public
speared with toothpicks
dusted with crushed powder,
dried plum.
You say sugarcane
is meant to be eaten
in the privacy of one's own room.

Flight

On a layover between Boston and California
I buy dried apricots for the time travel ahead
a shelf life outdating cartons of low-fat milk
or bags of stale potato chips

I pick up a copy of *Mademoiselle* to see what
the celebrities are wearing at this year's Oscar's
while clerks clear the stands of *The Daily Herald*
I hurry to catch a connecting flight, Terminal B

it is my father's voice I imagine lecturing me
on the causes of back strain caused by poor planning
why you must insist on carrying a whole life's worth
of belongings because there are always

these moments of separation
in freezing rain and fog the luggage
misrouted to Newark, New Jersey
the passengers grounded at O'Hare

temporary liberation from my possessions
the contents of the suitcase a copy
The Tibetan Book of Living & Dying
read in preparation for the end of a failing relationship,

a red alarm clock bargained for in Taiwan
a merchant surrounded in her stall by beeping clocks
drowned out in the clamor of a Taipei night market—
a photograph of a grandfather I never met, circa 1965,
the family garden at Ching Shui

the customer service agent assures me
melatonin works wonders for jetlag
and there is a world of difference
between "misplaced" and "lost"

I leave the counter with a claim ticket,
for a 1-800 number in Houston
share a cab on the expressway in a blizzard
with a lawyer with suites at the Knickerbocker,

looking up from the sidewalk at hotel lights
there is something more comforting
in sleeping in a bed strange with fresh linens
than coming home to a place where nothing
remains to be unpacked but memories.

Untitled

Before boarding each
flight to every foreign
place ventured,
I turn and see
my mother and father—
through tinted glass
of a partitioned gate,
their faces,
this continuity.

Elegy

for John Harvey Emett (1975-2002)

hallowed night,
a course of lanterns
wind down the

canyon road,
sand, wax,
brown paper,

farolitos, small
offerings, I will
raise and

light a lantern
for each year
of your absence,

a river
emptied out
to deepest seas,

the heart that
seeks,

release

The author would like to thank the editors of the following publications where some of these poems first appeared, sometimes in different versions: *Abroad View*: ""How to Eat Sugarcane" and "Sainte Terrer"; *After Hours*: "The Customer"; *Alphabet Faucet*: "A Type of Fish"; *Bostonia*: "The Gathering at the Orchid Pavilion"; *can we have our ball back?* : "A Fly Lands on the Great Eastern Sun", "It was a Clear Moonlit Night", "Jump", An Explanation of Magic"; *eye-rhyme*: "De Stijl", "Feedback", and "Yes Yoko Ono"; *Gumball Poetry*: "The Pilot"; *Mungo vs. Ranger*: "An Abbreviated History on the Way of Tea" and "Transience"; *The Poker*: "Recipe for Paper" and "Reel"; *Spinning Jenny*: "H"; "A Conversation between Huidobro and Braque" is reprinted from *Gastronomica*, Volume 2, No. 1, by permission of the University of California Press.

The author is grateful to The MacDowell Colony for providing the time and space to complete this manuscript. I am grateful for the support of many great mentors, teachers, and friends throughout the years. My deepest thanks to Andrew Schelling and John Cotter for providing editorial support. Special thanks to Kort Bergman.

COLOPHON

Set in CENTAUR,
designed by Bruce Rogers in 1912
as a prototype for an exclusive face to be
used by the Metropolitan Museum of Art.
Based on the roman letter of Nicolas Jenson,
this type evokes the high point of Venetian
printing. Frederic Warde cut a version of
Arrighi in 1929 for Monotype as a companion
and patterned it after the calligraphic
letterforms of Ludovico degli Arrighi,
an Italian writing teacher
of the 16th century.

•

Book design by J. Bryan

Shin Yu Pai grew up in
Southern California. She
studied at The Naropa
Institute and received a
MFA from the School of
the Art Institute of Chicago.
As a visual artist she has
exhibited her work at
galleries throughout the
Midwest and New England.
Equivalence is her first
full-length collection
of poetry.

PHOTOGRAPH—JOANNA ELDREDGE MORRISSEY